EASY TO MAKE

PRETTY THINGS
EASY TO MAKE
Hilary More

BROCKHAMPTON PRESS
LONDON

First published in Great Britain in 1989
by Anaya Publishers Ltd, Strode House,
44-50 Osnaburgh Street, London NW1 3ND
Reprinted 1990, 1991, 1992, 1993

This edition published 1996 by Brockhampton Press,
a member of Hodder Headline PLC Group

Editor Judith Casey
Design Rita Wüthrich
Photographer Paul Forrester
Illustrator Kate Simunek
Makes Originator Susan Macleod

British Library Cataloguing in Publication Data

More, Hilary
Pretty Things. – (Easy to make)
1. Handicrafts
I. Title II. Series
745.594

ISBN 1-86019-114-2

Typeset by Tradespools Limited, Frome, Somerset, UK
Printed and bound in EC

Introduction   6

NO-SEW CRAFTS

NEEDLECRAFTS

Introduction

*The increasing popularity of craft shops and craft fairs
is a clear sign that many of us love to give
and to receive specially chosen and individually made presents.*

A perfect present

What could be more exciting, and more rewarding, than making your own gifts for friends or family, each picked to match the recipient's character and taste. Most of these charming gift ideas are not only fun but also quick to make and involve few tools and only small quantities of materials.

Just for yourself

But the pretty things you make do not have to be reserved for others. Use up a leftover length of fabric or a roll of wallpaper to make yourself some of the delightfully decorative items shown here. Not only will they cost next to nothing but will provide your home with that cleverly co-ordinated look and personal touch that makes it look special.

This book sets out to inspire and successfully guide you through making **over 25** decorative items for yourself and for others. In this book you'll find:

● A photograph of each stunning article showing the finished result.

● A list of exactly what materials you need for each project, followed by clear step-by-step instructions that take you through from start to successful finish.

● Clear diagrams to match up with the instructions, help you to see how the item is made, and ensure a good result.

● Simple tips to help you avoid pitfalls and obtain a truly professional result. These furnish you with both the simple knowhow on modern techniques and provide you with the skills involved in traditional crafts.

● Simple projects taking only a minimum of time and money, leading on to the more complicated and beautiful items that you imagined only an expert could make. This allows those with only a little experience to gain confidence gradually.

● A source of inspiration for your own individual ideas. You can expand and develop some of the projects to give them your own personal touch.

● Two separate sections that make for easy reference.

Part 1 – No-sew crafts

This section involves no sewing whatsoever. Instead it covers ingenious ways of cutting, wrapping, covering and glueing paper, card and fabric to provide a wide range of decorative items such as a smart desk set complete with covered books and files – ideal for the budding writer. We show you the easiest way to frame your loved ones' photographs or to give a mirror an attractive border. There are also unusual lampshades and waste bins; even cookie tins are given a lift with the addition of fabric. To finish this part of the book there is a stunning picture made from leftover fabric glued onto a plain background – if you cannot draw then this must be the best way to create a masterpiece.

Materials include colourful wrapping papers, cards you hate to throw away, lengths of wallpaper and both dressmaking and furnishing fabrics as well as ribbon, lace and other scraps, plus card and common household items. Involve the children in some of these projects. They will enjoy learning new skills and the next rainy day could be transformed into a delightful and rewarding time.

Part 2 – Needlecrafts

The second half of the book is designed to build up from projects involving only the simplest stitchwork, so that even a novice can enjoy successful results. You'll then have the confidence to go on to the more complicated but highly decorative heirloom items.

This section starts with instructions for making perennial favourites such as sachets for sweet smelling pot pourri, and covered coat hangers, and goes on to include curtain tie-backs, and tablecloths for turning dark corners into interesting focal points. The most time-consuming but very special gifts are the attractively-designed patchwork star and baby quilt that end the book. You'll find something to make, even if you only have a short time to spare or, several winter evenings to extend your knowledge and skill.

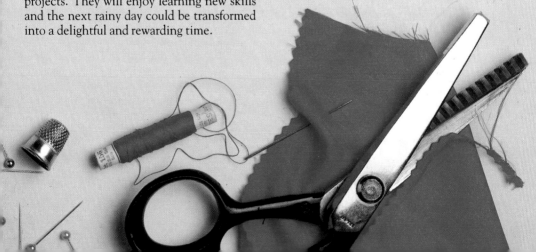

1: NO-SEW CRAFTS

Write minded

Give yourself the accessories in which to pen that bestseller –
a matching desk set. Underneath is the blotter, made from coloured
card, while the holders are covered in distinctive wrapping paper.
Most work stations are sombre places so why not treat yourself
to a new desk set to encourage you to write that great work.

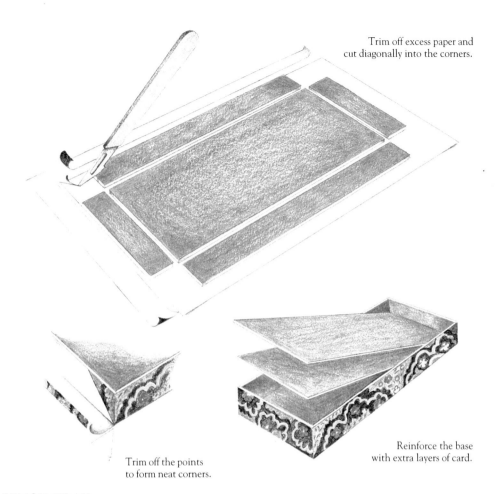

Trim off excess paper and cut diagonally into the corners.

Trim off the points to form neat corners.

Reinforce the base with extra layers of card.

PENCIL TRAY

Materials
Thick coloured card 12×8in (30×20cm)
Wrapping paper 11×6in (28×15cm)
Paper adhesive
Craft scissors and sharp craft knife

To make pencil tray
1 From card cut out a piece 7³/₄×3in (19.5×7.5cm) for base. Cut two long sides each 7³/₄×⁷/₈in (19.5×2cm) and two short sides each 3×⁷/₈in (7.5×2cm).

2 Lay the wrapping paper right side down. Apply adhesive on one side of card base and stick centrally to paper. Repeat, to stick long sides on either side of base and then short sides. Leave a gap between each piece, the width of the card thickness.

3 Trim along outer edges of side pieces, continuing at each corner until cut edges meet. Then cut diagonally into each corner up to corner of base.

4 Bring up the long sides, then the short sides. Trim and tuck edges of paper on long sides under paper on short sides, stick. Trim edges on short sides level with tray edge and stick in place.

5 To reinforce the base, cut two more pieces of card slightly smaller than base and stick inside tray.

PEN/PENCIL HOLDER

Materials
Wrapping paper 17 × 14in (43 × 36cm)
Thick coloured card 15 × 9in
   (38 × 22.5cm)
Paper adhesive
Craft scissors and sharp craft knife

To make pen holder
1 Make up three sections. For the tallest
section cut two pieces of card 2in (5cm)
wide and two pieces of card 1⅞in (4cm)
wide, by 5in (12.5cm) long. For the two
smaller sections, cut card to the same width
but 4in (10cm) and 1in (2.5cm) long.

2 Lay the wrapping paper right side down on
a flat surface. Stick the card pieces side by
side on the paper, with the space between
each piece the thickness of the card. Trim
paper to within 1in (2.5cm) of card on side
edges. Trim paper level with card on top and
base edges.

3 Roll up each holder and stick down, so the
paper join is in the centre of one side.

4 Stick the holders together, with seams
hidden on the inside.

5 For base, cut out a 4¾in (12cm) square of
card. Cut a square of paper the same size.
Stick paper to one side of card, the
underneath.

6 Stick holders centrally to uncovered side
of base.

7 Cut strips of card to fit the spaces between
holders and outer edge. Stick in place, to aid
stability.

> To make the tray and pen/pencil holder
> easy to clean, cover with a clear sticky-
> backed plastic, in the same way as with
> the paper.
>
> Fix a square of blotting paper inside the
> tall pen/pencil holders, to catch any inky
> leaks.

Stick alternate widths of card
side by side on the paper.

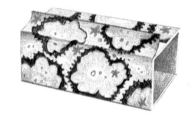

Position paper join centrally
on one side of each holder.

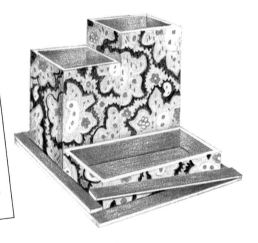

Add card strips between
holders and outer edge.

BLOTTER

Materials
Thick coloured card 22in (56cm) square
Paper adhesive
Sharp craft knife
Blotting paper 20¹/₄ × 15¹/₄in (51 × 39cm)

To make blotter
1 Cut one piece of card 21 × 16in
(53 × 41cm). For corners cut two squares 4in
(10cm). Cut each square in half diagonally
to form four triangles.

2 Make up each corner in the same way: cut
³/₈in (1cm) wide strips of card and stick to
wrong side of each triangle along the two
straight edges. Trim off ends diagonally to
match corner pieces. Stick corner pieces in
place, by sticking down strip sections only,
making sure that outer edges match. Insert
blotting paper.

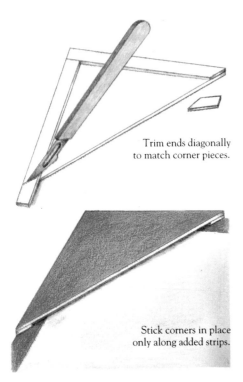

Trim ends diagonally
to match corner pieces.

Stick corners in place
only along added strips.

Under wraps

Give your favourite books a face-lift with a new cover.
Nowadays with a huge range of wrapping paper on the market,
you will be spoilt for choice.
Mix and match is the answer.

Materials

To cover two books: $6\frac{1}{2}$in (16.5cm) square
and $6 \times 3\frac{1}{2}$in (15×9cm)
Wrapping paper $14 \times 7\frac{1}{2}$in (35.5×19cm)
and 8×7in (20×18cm)
Spray adhesive
Craft scissors and sharp craft knife

To cover the books

1 Cover each book in the same way. Lay the wrapping paper right side down on a flat surface, spray with adhesive.

2 Position open book with one edge to within $\frac{1}{2}$in (13mm) of one short side. Make sure that the book is at right angles to the paper edge. Close the book. Carefully smooth the paper over the front cover.

3 Run a finger nail down spine to crease the paper, and continue sticking paper round the back cover.

4 At the spine, open book and cut overlapping paper into Vs. Push inside spine.

5 Cut the overlapping paper across the corners; fold remaining edges to inside and stick in place, forming neat corners.

You can cover any book in the same way, just make sure you allow enough give round the spine.

Smooth paper over the book cover.

Push Vs up inside the spine.

Stick the overlaps in place.

Box clever

Gone are the days when you kept bills in an old envelope
in the kitchen drawer. Today you can choose colourful wrapping paper
and make yourself a set of designer box files to display.
Match the files to your office area or, as they look so good,
sneak them into the bookcase.

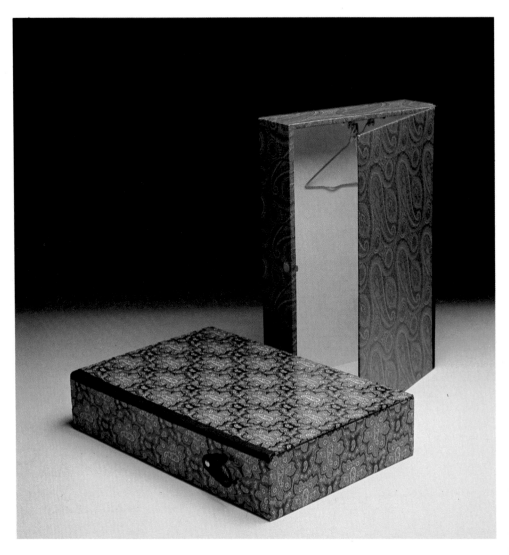

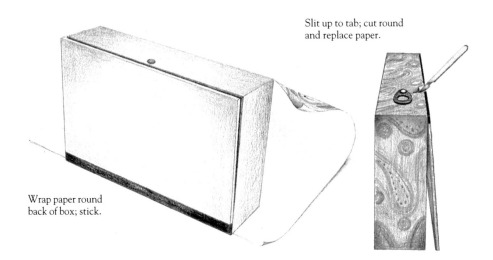

Slit up to tab; cut round and replace paper.

Wrap paper round back of box; stick.

Materials
A4 box file, $14^1/_2 \times 9^1/_2 \times 3$in
   ($36.5 \times 24 \times 7.5$ cm) deep
Wrapping paper $32 \times 16^1/_2$in (81×42 cm)
Spray adhesive
Craft scissors and sharp craft knife

To cover box file
1 Cut a piece of paper $22 \times 16^1/_2$in
(56×42cm). Reserve rest of paper.

2 Lay wrapping paper right side down on a flat surface and spray with adhesive. Lay box file centrally on paper with one short edge butting against back hinge. Smooth paper round body of file to opposite side.

3 Cut diagonally into paper at front corners and fold in top and base edges. Stick in place. Trim off excess paper at front corners.

4 Turn in paper along front edge, trimming paper, so it matches front edge. Stick in place with edge to inside.

5 Using sharp craft knife cut round button.

6 At back tab, cut into paper at right angles to base, up to tab, and then cut out circle to fit round tab. Stick and smooth paper back in place.

7 For lid, cut a piece of paper 10×16in (25×40.5cm). Spray with adhesive as before, and stick to lid, butting left-hand edge against back hinge and with an equal amount of overlap at top and base edges.

8 Snip into front corners and stick overlap to inside of box, trimming round the catch.

Make sure that the paper is cut and stuck on the box file with the design running straight.

Make covered name tags for the spine of the box: cut a piece of sticky-backed plastic $2^1/_2 \times 1^1/_2$in (6.5×4cm). Write the contents on a piece of card 2×1in (5×2.5cm). Place card centrally behind plastic and stick edges of plastic to spine of box file.

Alternatively cover each file with a different wrapping paper.

Make sure that your craft knife is sharp before trimming round the front button and back tab.

Hat trick

Keep up with tradition and transform a plain hat
box into an elegant piece of luggage.
Even if you never wear a hat,
why not use this attractively-shaped box to store your love letters?

Materials

One hat box 6in (15cm) deep and 10½in
   (26.5cm) in diameter
Wrapping paper 34×22in (87×56cm)
Ruler
Spray adhesive
Craft scissors and sharp craft knife

To cover a hat box

1 Remove the lid and measure the
circumference of the box, adding 1in
(2.5cm) for join. Cut paper to this length by
the depth of the box plus 1in (2.5cm).

2 Lay the paper right side down on a flat
surface and spray with adhesive. Carefully
lay the side of the box centrally on the paper
at right angles to one end. Roll the paper
round the box, smoothing out any air
bubbles and creases. Overlap and stick down
the ends. To achieve a good butt join, place
a ruler over the join of double paper and
carefully run a sharp craft knife down against
the ruler. Peel away the excess paper.

3 At the base, snip into overlap of paper at
½in (13mm) intervals all round the box.
Stick overlaps in place to base.

4 At top, turn overlap to the inside of the
box and stick in place, forming small evenly-
spaced tucks, if necessary, to pleat away
excess paper.

5 For outside base, cut out a circle of paper,
slightly smaller than diameter of box base.
Stick to base covering raw edges.

6 For lid top, cut a circle of paper ¾in (2cm)
larger than diameter of lid. Stick lid
centrally to wrong side of paper. Snip into
overlap at ½in (1.3cm) intervals all round.
Stick overlap down onto sides.

7 To cover lid sides, measure circumference
of lid and cut out one strip to this length plus
1in (2.5cm) for joins, by just under twice
the lid depth.

8 Stick strip to lid side, over raw edges,
placing top edge of strip to top edge of lid.
Stick overlap to inside of lid.

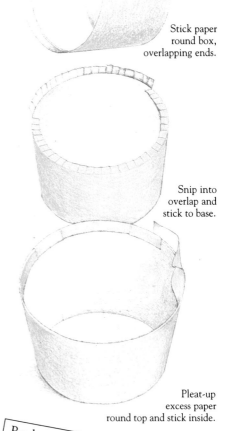

Stick paper
round box,
overlapping ends.

Snip into
overlap and
stick to base.

Pleat-up
excess paper
round top and stick inside.

Replace the lid so that the joins on the
lid and box fall in the same place.

If possible position joins over an original
join on the box.

Add a carrying cord – punch a hole 1¾in
(4.5cm) down on opposite sides of the
box. Remove the lid. Thread the ends of
a 26in (66cm) length of cord through
both holes and knot inside the box,
leaving a loop on the outside. Replace
the lid.

Light work

Distinctive marbled paper in rich red and swirls of gold
transforms this plain shade into a leading light.
Add matching decorative braids to complete the ensemble.
This shade would look perfect in a study,
mixed and matched with a whole host of other rich furnishing hues.

Materials

Bought shade 8¹/₂in (21.5cm) high with
   11¹/₂in (29cm) diameter base and 6in
   (15cm) diameter top
2 standard sheets of marbled wrapping paper
Wooden clothes pegs
Brown paper for pattern
⁵/₈yd (60cm) of ¹/₂in (13mm) wide decorative
   trimming
1¹/₈yd (1m) of 2in (5cm) wide decorative
   fringe trimming
Spray and clear adhesives
Sharp craft knife

To cover shade

1 Draw a line down the shade at the
positions of bulb fixings, to mark side seam
positions. Check each half is the same size.

2 Peg the piece of brown paper over one half
of the shade. Using a pencil, mark the
outline of the shade on the paper. Remove
from shade and cut out.

3 Using the brown paper pattern, cut out
two pieces of marbled paper, adding a scant
¹/₂in (13mm) all round.

4 Spray adhesive on the wrong side of one
piece of paper. Line up the edge ¹/₂in
(13mm) over the marked side seam on
lampshade and stick in place.

5 Stick second half of shade in place
overlapping the first one at sides.

6 To achieve a good butt join, run a craft
knife down the side seams, through both
layers of paper, remove excess paper.

7 Trim off top and base edges against top
and base edges of lampshade.

8 Cut decorative trimming to fit round top
edge and dip ends into adhesive to seal.
Stick trimming round top edge, slightly
overlapping the top edge of shade and
placing seam over one of the paper seams.

9 Cut fringe trim, seal ends then stick round
base edge, slightly overlapping shade.

Mark the shade outlines on the
wrong side of wrapping paper.

Match up the paper edges
to the side seams on basic shade.

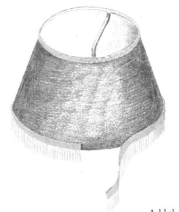

Add the base
fringe trimming
after sealing the ends.

Photo call

Frame the photos of your loved ones in a pretty print fabric.
The basic shape is cut from card and softly padded with wadding.
At the back a simple stand is anchored in place. You can make
the frame to any size, with a square, rectangular
or circular centre to suit the shape of the photograph.

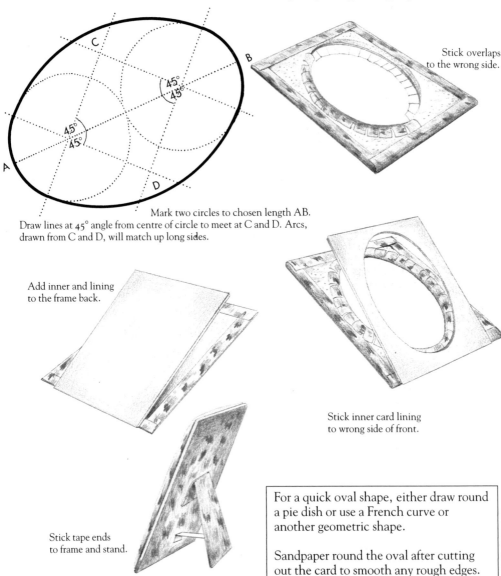

Stick overlaps
to the wrong side.

Mark two circles to chosen length AB.
Draw lines at 45° angle from centre of circle to meet at C and D. Arcs,
drawn from C and D, will match up long sides.

Add inner and lining
to the frame back.

Stick inner card lining
to wrong side of front.

Stick tape ends
to frame and stand.

For a quick oval shape, either draw round
a pie dish or use a French curve or
another geometric shape.

Sandpaper round the oval after cutting
out the card to smooth any rough edges.

Materials

Thick card 16×6in (40.5×15cm)
Thin card 9×7in (23×18cm)
Printed cotton fabric 14×12in
 (35.5×30cm)
Lightweight wadding 6½×5in
 (16.5×12.5cm)
Fabric adhesive
Wooden clothes pegs
4in (10cm) of ½in (13mm) wide tape
Scissors and craft knife

To make photo frame

1 From thick card cut two pieces each
6½×5in (16.5×12.5cm) for frame.

2 Make a pattern for an oval about 5×3¼in
(12.5×8cm) on spare paper, following the
diagram. Cut out pattern. Position to centre
of frame front and draw round. Cut out.

3 Stick wadding to one side of front. Cut out
the centre oval and discard.

4 Cut a piece of fabric 7½×6in (19×15cm).
Lay the fabric with right side down on a flat
surface; stick wadded side of frame front
centrally to wrong side of fabric. Bring raw
edges to wrong side and stick in place. Cut
round the oval centre, leaving about ¾in
(2cm) turning beyond the oval. Snip into
this fabric and stick to wrong side.

5 Cover the remaining piece of thick card
with fabric for frame back; omit wadding.

6 For backing pieces, cut two pieces of thin
card 6¼×4½in (16×11.5cm). Stick one
piece centrally to inside of back, matching
base edges only. Place second piece centrally
to wrong side of front, matching base edges
only. Mark round oval. Remove from frame
and cut out oval ¼in (6mm) larger than
frame oval and discard. Stick backing to
wrong side of front, centrally with only base
edges matching.

7 To stick front frame to back, apply a layer
of adhesive round the frame edge, making
sure the backing card is free from glue. Press
frame together and hold with wooden
clothes pegs while drying.

8 For the stand, cut a piece of thick card
3¼×2½in (8×6cm). Mark the centre of
stand lengthways. Mark 1in (2.5cm) on
either side of centre line. Join up these
marks to opposite corners. Cut along these
diagonal lines to shape the stand.

9 Cut a piece of fabric 12×3in (30×7.5cm).
Stick top of stand to within ¼in (6mm) of
one end of fabric. Trim side edges to ¼in
(6mm) and turn in over stand to opposite
side and stick in place. Turn up fabric over
uncovered side of stand, trimming and
tucking under side edges in line with card
edges; stick in place.

10 Trim off excess fabric on stand to within
2in (5cm) of card top. Fold this flap of fabric
in half and stick together.

11 Line up the base of the stand with the
frame and mark position of top of stand.
Stick flap of stand to back of frame at this
mark with stand above the flap. Leave to
dry. Bring the stand down over flap of fabric.

12 Turn under tape ends for ½in (13mm)
and stick ½in (13mm) up from base edge
with one end to stand and one end to back
of frame.

On reflection

Take a simple mirror tile and turn it into a pretty hanging mirror with wadding and print fabric.
Once covered, you can leave the surround plain or add decorative cords, braids, sequins or bows, whatever takes your fancy.

Materials
Thick card 24 × 11 in (61 × 28cm)
Cotton fabric 23 × 12 in (58 × 30cm)
9in (23cm) square mirror tile
Wadding 10½in (26.5cm) square
12in (30cm) length of cord, for hanging
¾yd (70cm) length of decorative cord
Fabric adhesive
Pair of compasses
Darning needle
Wooden clothes pegs
Scissors and craft knife

To make framed mirror
1 From thick card cut two pieces each 10½in (26.5cm) square. Mark the centre of one piece, the front, by drawing intersecting lines diagonally from corner to corner. Using compasses, mark an 8in (20cm) circle centrally; cut out and discard.

2 Stick wadding to one side of front. Cut out central hole from wadding and discard.

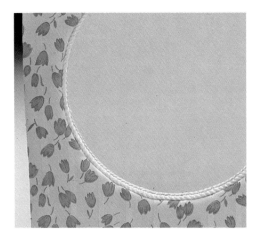

3 Cut an 11in (28cm) square of fabric and lay right side down on a flat surface. Stick wadded side of card centrally to fabric. Bring raw edges to wrong side and stick in place. Cut out central hole leaving ¾in (2cm) turning. Snip into this fabric and stick to wrong side of frame.

4 Peel off sticky pads on the back of the mirror tile. Stick tile centrally to frame back. Cut ½in (13mm) wide strips of card and matching outer edges, stick to edge of frame back, around the mirror tile until the sides are the same thickness as the tile.

5 Make two holes for hanging cord on either side of tile, ¾in (2cm) in from each side edge and 4in (10cm) down from top edge.

6 Cut an 11in (28cm) square of fabric. Lay the fabric right side down on a flat surface. Stick back of mirror card centrally to fabric. Bring raw edges to mirror side of card and stick down. Trim off fabric round mirror tile.

7 Turn card over, feel for holes and using sharp darning needle pierce fabric. Thread cord through holes, so it is taut across back. Knot ends on the inside; tuck into the card strips at each side and stick in place.

8 Stick frame front over mirror back, matching outer edges exactly. Hold with wooden clothes pegs or place under heavy books while the frame is drying.

9 Seal the ends of the decorative cord by dipping them in fabric adhesive. Stick decorative cord round the inner circle, positioning seam in centre of base of circle.

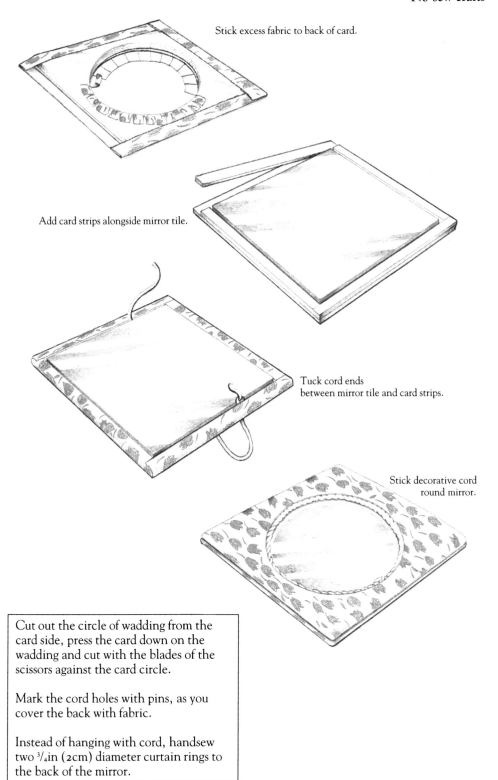

Stick excess fabric to back of card.

Add card strips alongside mirror tile.

Tuck cord ends
between mirror tile and card strips.

Stick decorative cord
round mirror.

Cut out the circle of wadding from the
card side, press the card down on the
wadding and cut with the blades of the
scissors against the card circle.

Mark the cord holes with pins, as you
cover the back with fabric.

Instead of hanging with cord, handsew
two $^3/_4$in (2cm) diameter curtain rings to
the back of the mirror.

Tissue transformation

Disguise a shop-bought tissue box with a snazzy padded cover.
The basic cover is made of card, with layers of wadding and fabric.
Make one to match each bedroom, using remnants of furnishing fabric.
Tie in with the cotton wool holder for a co-ordinated set.

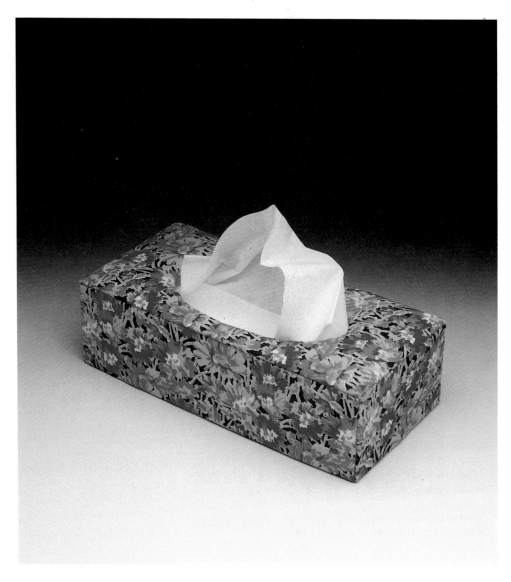

Materials

Thick card 15 × 12in (38 × 30cm)
Lightweight wadding 11 × 5in (28 × 12.5cm)
Furnishing fabric 22 × 14in (56 × 35.5cm)
Box of tissues
Fabric adhesive
Sharp craft knife and scissors

To make the tissue box cover

1 From card cut one piece $10^1/_4 \times 4^3/_4$in
(26×12cm) for top, two pieces each
$4^3/_4 \times 2^3/_4$in (12×7cm) for short sides and two
pieces each $2^3/_4 \times 10^1/_4$in (7×26cm) for long
sides.

2 Remove the oval from the box of tissues
and use as a template. Place centrally on
card top and draw round. Using a sharp craft
knife carefully cut out oval and discard.

3 Using card as a template, cut a piece of
wadding the same size as top, stick to one
side of card top. Cut out oval from wadding
to match card and discard.

4 Cut a piece of fabric 1in (2.5cm) larger all
round than top section. Lay fabric right side
down on a flat surface, stick wadded section
centrally on top. Bring raw fabric edges over
to wrong side and stick in place, forming
neat corners. Cut out centre of oval, leaving
a border of about $^3/_4$in (2cm) around oval.
Snip into this border all round at about $^1/_2$in
(13mm) intervals and stick to wrong side.

5 Cover the remaining pieces of card with
fabric only. Place fabric pieces right side
down, stick card centrally to wrong side.
Turn raw edges over to wrong side and stick
in place, forming neat corners.

6 Place top section right side down on a flat
surface. Stick long sides to edge, then the
two short side pieces, slotting them in
between the long sections. Check that all
edges butt together before leaving to dry.

When cutting shaped areas from card,
run the craft knife carefully round the
shape to create a groove, then go over the
shape again, in the groove, this time
pressing hard enough to cut the card.

Add extra fabric adhesive inside the
cover to make the joins extra firm.

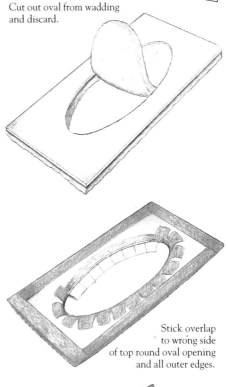

Cut out oval from wadding
and discard.

Stick overlap
to wrong side
of top round oval opening
and all outer edges.

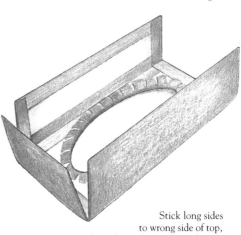

Stick long sides
to wrong side of top,
then slot in short sides and stick.

Trinket box

Keep all your secrets locked away in this decoupage trinket box.
The domed lid is covered in flower heads,
while the inside is lined and softly padded.
We've kept the decoration unsealed, to give a more raised effect.

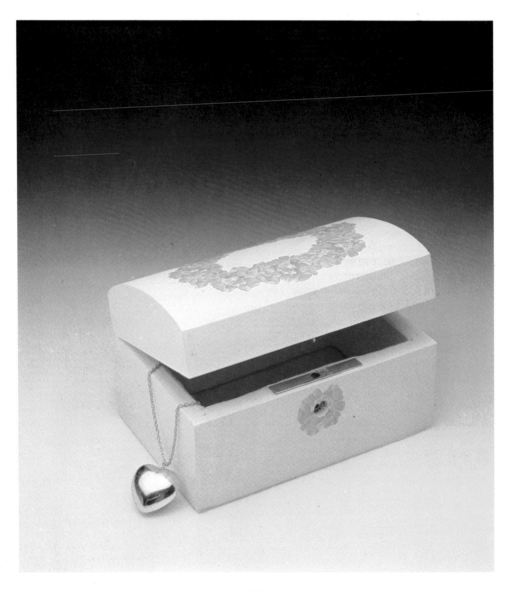

Materials

Dome-shaped hinged wooden box,
   $5^{1}/_{2} \times 3^{1}/_{2} \times 3^{1}/_{4}$in ($14 \times 9 \times 8$cm) deep
Matt white spray paint
Sheet of floral wrapping paper
Clear adhesive
White felt 12×6in (30×15cm)
Plain cotton fabric 10×7in (25×17.5cm)
Lightweight wadding the same size as fabric
Thin card 7×6in (17.5×15cm)
Sharp craft knife and scissors

To decorate trinket box

1 Spray paint the box, outside and inside.
Leave to dry.

2 Carefully cut flower heads from wrapping
paper. Arrange flower heads in an oval ring
on top of the lid and when the arrangement
looks good, stick in place.

3 Stick one flower head over the keyhole in
the front of the box. Cut out the keyhole.

4 Measure the inside of the box and cut a
piece of white felt to fit each side. Stick felt
in place.

5 Measure inside the lid and cut a piece of
thin card to this size. Using card as a
template, cut one piece of wadding the same
size. Cut a piece of fabric 1in (2.5cm) larger
all round than the card.

6 Stick wadding to one side of card. Place
fabric right side down on a flat surface. Stick
wadded side of card centrally to wrong side
of fabric. Turn and stick raw edges to wrong
side of card. Stick padded lid lining in place.

7 Repeat, to make a padded base for the
inside of the box in the same way.

8 Cut a piece of felt $5^{1}/_{2} \times 3^{1}/_{2}$in ($14 \times 9$cm).
Stick to underside of box.

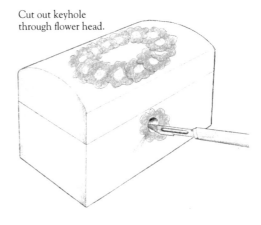

Cut out keyhole
through flower head.

Stick padded
lid lining in place
inside box.

Run an emery board over the painted
surface before sticking the flowers in
place, to provide a key for the adhesive.

Decorate the key to match the box. Cut a
5in (12.5cm) length of ribbon and thread
through key end. Using a paper flower
head as a template, cut out two pieces of
pink felt the same shape. Stick the felt
flower heads together sandwiching ribbon
ends in between.

Floral arrangement

Design your own still-life without drawing a line.
All you need to do is cut out lots of different flower shapes
to create a collage you'll be proud to hang on the wall.
Take the same idea to create a landscape picture of flowers in a garden.

Materials
Backing card 21 × 17¹/₂in (53 × 44.5cm)
Background fabric, the same size as card
Spray adhesive
Offcut of floral fabric
Striped fabric for vase
Thin card 6in (15cm) square
Paper for pattern
Fabric adhesive
Sharp fabric scissors

To make the collage
1 Iron background fabric and using spray adhesive, fix to backing card, matching outer edges.

2 Cut out flowers and leaves from floral fabric.

3 Position flowers and leaves on background fabric and roughly arrange as a bunch. Decide on the size and shape of the vase – ours was about 5¹/₂ × 4in (14 × 10cm) – and roughly cut a piece of paper to that size. Fold in half lengthways. Draw out one half of vase shape freehand. Keeping the paper folded, cut out the vase shape. Unfold.

4 Using paper pattern cut out a vase shape from thin card.

5 Cut out ⁵/₈in (1.5cm) wide strips from striped fabric and weave together over card vase; stick in place. Turn card over and trim off fabric to match card outline.

6 Stick vase centrally to background fabric, 2in (5cm) up from base edge.

7 Rearrange flowers and leaves over background fabric, around vase, until the arrangement looks good, then carefully lift each piece in turn and stick in place with fabric adhesive. If necessary, mark positions of motifs as you lift them with pins, so they can be replaced in the exact position.

8 Leave to dry, then frame.

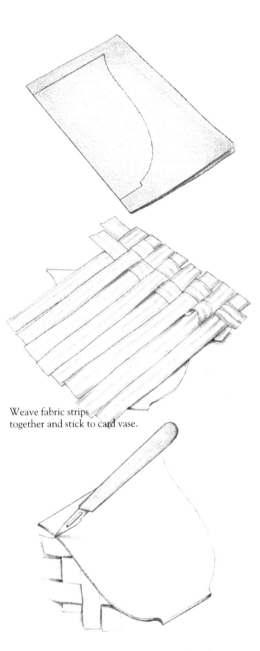

Draw vase freehand for the pattern.

Weave fabric strips together and stick to card vase.

Turn card over and trim round edge of vase.

Waste not want not

*Upgrade a boring metal or plastic wastepaper bin with smart fabric
and decorative cord.
You'll find it quick and easy to cover, whatever the size of the basic bin,
so you can make one for every room
where the waste paper threatens to take over.*

Materials

Piece of furnishing fabric 40×25in
  (102×63cm)
1¹/₄yd (1.5m) of decorative cord
Metal or plastic bin, 10in (25.5cm) high
Spray and fabric adhesives
Wooden clothes pegs
Braid (circumference of small tin + turn-
  under)

To cover the wastepaper bin

1 Measure the circumference at the widest
part of the bin. Cut a piece of fabric to this
length plus 2in (5cm), by the depth of the
bin plus 2in (5cm).

Cut the fabric edge straight in line with seam on bin.

2 Temporarily hold the fabric to bin with
wooden clothes pegs and trim fabric to
within 1in (2.5cm) of edges.

3 Spray the wrong side of fabric at one end
with adhesive and place on the bin at the
bin seam. Cut along the fabric in a straight
line, using the bin seam as a guide.

4 Continue spraying the fabric with
adhesive and smoothing it round the bin,
eliminating any air bubbles or creases. Trim
off the opposite edge straight, allowing a ¹/₄in
(6mm) overlap. Trim overlap and stick in
place.

Trim off base edge, just above rim.

5 Trim off excess fabric at top and bottom
just under bim rims.

6 Dip cut end of cord in fabric adhesive to
seal. Stick cord round top edge of bin,
covering raw edge of fabric and trim other
end of cord, so ends butt together. Dip
remaining end in fabric adhesive to seal.
Stick cord in place.

7 Repeat with cord at base edge of bin.

8 Cover the centre section only of the small
bin and trim with braid. Stick braid over raw
edges of fabric in same way as cord.

Seal ends and stick cord in place round top and base.

Bins can be covered with wallpaper to
match the room's décor in the same way.

Cookie time

Brighten up the kitchen with a row of fabric covered cookie tins.
Use a fabric remnant leftover from the kitchen curtains
or just pick a printed fabric that fits in with the colour scheme.
We domed the top with wadding
and added a smart braid round the lid.

Materials

Tin, 6in (15cm) high, 4¹/₂in (11.5cm) in diameter
Small amount of emulsion paint and brush
Fabric 15in (38cm) square
Lightweight wadding 12×6 in (30×15cm)
¹/₂yd (40cm) of ³/₈in (1cm) wide braid
Spray and fabric adhesives

To cover cookie tin

1 Paint tin with emulsion paint, to cover any blemishes. Leave to dry.

2 Cut a circle of wadding the same size as lid, plus a circle of wadding ³/₄in (2cm) smaller than lid. With fabric adhesive, stick small circle of wadding centrally to lid, then cover with larger circle of wadding, to create a domed effect. Leave to dry.

3 Cut a circle of fabric 1in (2.5cm) larger than lid. Centrally place fabric right side up over wadded lid. Pull fabric firmly over lid and stick to the lid edge at opposite sides. Repeat at right angles to first points.

4 Work round the lid sticking fabric at opposite sides. Snip small Vs into overlap to take away excess fabric, making sure fabric is smooth. Trim off fabric above tin rim.

5 Cut a length of braid to fit round lid. Dip braid ends into fabric adhesive to seal the ends. Stick braid round edge of lid, butting edges together.

6 Put lid on tin. Measure round tin for length of fabric, adding an extra 1in (2.5cm). Measure from lid edge to base adding an extra 1in (2.5cm). Cut a piece of fabric to this size.

7 Spray fabric with adhesive and stick one short edge to seam on tin. Continue sticking fabric round tin, turning under ¹/₂in (13mm) at top and base edges. Turn under opposite raw edge and stick over raw edge at seam.

Dome the lid with two layers of wadding.

Snip into fabric to achieve a smooth fit.

Turn under all the raw edges and stick to tin.

When you've covered your tin with fabric, spray with a protective coating to help keep the fabric clean.

2: NEEDLECRAFTS

Cushioned for comfort

*Add the final touch to a room with a collection of
decorative cushions, plain or ruffled. They'll
bring a sofa to life, take the hard edge off wooden or wicker chairs
and bring the pleasing addition of colour to a neutral décor.*

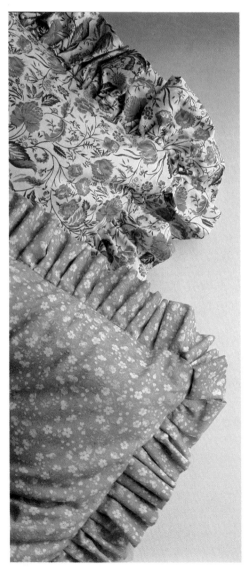

Materials
1yd (1m) of 36in (90cm) wide printed
    furnishing fabric
15in (38cm) square cushion pad
15in (38cm) zip
Matching sewing thread

To make a ruffled cushion
1 For cover front cut one piece of printed
fabric 16$\frac{1}{4}$in (41cm) square. For cover back
cut one piece 16$\frac{1}{4} \times 8\frac{3}{4}$in (41 × 22cm) for
left-hand section and one piece 16$\frac{1}{4} \times 9$in
(41 × 23cm) for right-hand section.

2 For ruffle, cut out sufficient 6in (15cm)
wide crossway strips, which, when stitched
together will be twice the length of the outer
edge of cover front – 130in (330cm).

3 Turn under one edge of left-hand back
section for $\frac{5}{8}$in (1.5cm) and press; place
against the zip teeth; baste and stitch, using
a zipper foot on the sewing machine.

4 Turn under one edge of right-hand back
section for 1in (2.5cm) and press. Overlap
this edge over zip teeth and left-hand edge
for $\frac{1}{8}$in (3mm); baste and stitch, using zipper
foot on the sewing machine. Baste across
ends of zip.

5 Pin and stitch the ruffle strips together to
form a ring, with plain flat seams, taking $\frac{5}{8}$in
(1.5cm) seam allowance. Trim and press
seams open. Fold ruffle in half lengthways,
wrong sides together.

6 Divide ruffle into four equal sections and mark with pins. Work two rows of gathering stitches $5/8$in (1.5cm) from raw edges in each section of ruffle, beginning and ending stitching at marking pins.

7 Mark the centre of each cushion side with a pin.

8 Position ruffle to right side of cushion front, with ruffle facing inwards, gathering $5/8$in (1.5cm) from outer edge and matching marking pins together. Pull up the gathering stitches evenly in each section in turn, allowing extra gathers at each corner. Pin gathers in place. Check that the gathers are even, then baste and stitch all round cover, $5/8$in (1.5cm) from outer edge.

9 Open zip. Place cover back to cover front with right sides together, enclosing ruffle, matching outer edges. Pin and stitch all round cover, following previous line of stitches.

10 Trim and zigzag stitch raw edges together. Turn cover to right side through zip. Insert cushion pad and close zip.

Before stitching cover front to back, pin ruffle edges to cushion front, so they will not get caught up in the stitching, when the cover pieces are joined together.

Add a double ruffle quickly and easily by inserting a length of pre-gathered broderie anglaise between the cushion front and main ruffle.

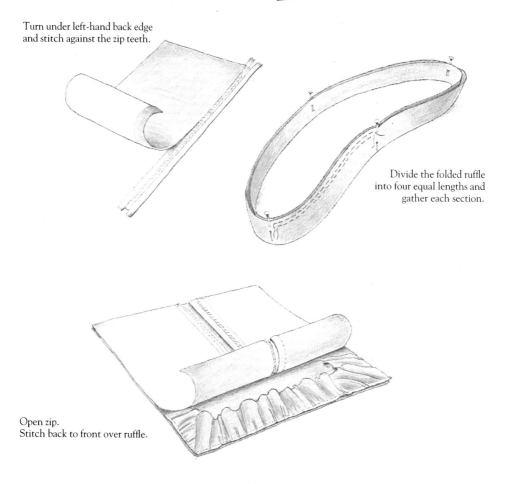

Turn under left-hand back edge and stitch against the zip teeth.

Divide the folded ruffle into four equal lengths and gather each section.

Open zip.
Stitch back to front over ruffle.

Circular tablecloths

*Hide a plain round table with a floor-length circular cloth
and turn it into the focal point of a room.
We kept the main cloth plain and made the top cloth out of lace
looped up at the sides with ribbon bows. Simply thread ribbon
through holes in the lace and tie in bows around the edge.*

Materials

Furnishing cotton fabric or lace, see below
　　for amount
Matching sewing thread
Paper, string and drawing pin for pattern
Scissors

To make the circular tablecloth

1 Measure the diameter of the table top and
the desired length. To calculate the
diameter of the cloth, add twice the table
height to the diameter of the table top, plus
$\frac{1}{2}$in (13mm) for hem.

2 Cut a sheet of paper slightly larger than
one quarter of the cloth. Cut a length of
string 10in (25.5cm) longer than half the
diameter of the cloth. Tie one end of the
string round the pointed end of a pencil. Pin
the other end of string to one corner of the
paper, with the string the exact length of
half of the cloth diameter. Draw an arc from
one side of the paper to the other, keeping
the string taut and holding the drawing pin.
Cut out the resulting pattern.

3 Fold the fabric in half and then in half
again in the opposite direction. Position the
paper with corners matching, cut out the
tablecloth. Unfold the fabric.

4 Turn under a double $\frac{1}{4}$in (6mm) wide hem
all round the outer edge of cloth. Pin, baste
and stitch hem in place.

To add ribbons: cut six 30in (76cm)
lengths of $\frac{1}{4}$in (6mm) wide ribbon. Mark
the outer edge of cloth into six equal
sections. Thread ribbon through lace and
over outer edge and tie into bows.

If the fabric is not wide enough to cut the
cloth in one piece, seam two fabric
widths together with flat fell seams. Cut
one fabric width in half lengthways and
seam to either side of one full-width
piece, so there will not be an unsightly
seam running across the table top.

Holding drawing pin
firmly in corner draw an arc
from side to side across the paper.

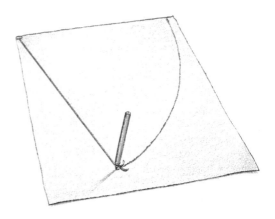

Cut out tablecloth
using the quarter paper pattern.

A touch of lace

Lower the lights and see the effect of a pretty lace lampshade.

Because of its romantic, timeless feel,

lace is always a favourite for soft furnishings.

Here it has been gathered and used to cover a plain lampshade,

so you can glimpse the design illuminated by the soft light.

Materials

Bought coolie lampshade, 8¹/₂in (21.5cm)
high, 15in (38cm) diameter base and 4in
(10cm) diameter top

1¹/₂yd (1.4m) of 12in (30cm) wide self-edged
lace

Paper for pattern

Plain cotton fabric and sewing thread

Spray fabric adhesive

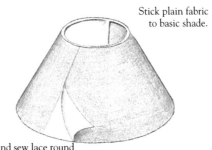

Stick plain fabric
to basic shade.

Hand sew lace round
top edge of shade.

To make lace-covered lampshade

1 Make up a pattern for the lampshade as for
the marbled shade (see page 25). Cut out
each piece from plain fabric. Spray shade
with adhesive and lay fabric pieces on top,
positioning two seams on either side of shade
at positions of light fixings.

2 Seam lace together with a narrow French
seam.

3 Work two rows of gathering stitches 2in
(5cm) down from top edge of lace. Pull up
stitches to fit top of shade, positioning seam
over one of the seams on shade. Handsew in
place through gathering stitches.

Étui box

Based on a Chinese concept of a box within a box,
this étui is a small self-contained needlework box,
made up of fabric-covered card leaves which,
when the lid is removed, open out to reveal all your sewing needs.
Étuis were first made by soldiers and seamen in the 19th century.

Needlecrafts

Materials

Printed cotton fabric 28$\frac{1}{2}$ × 11$\frac{1}{2}$in
   (72.5 × 29cm)
Plain fabric 10 × 8in (25 × 20cm)
Thick card 18 × 11in (46 × 28cm)
Thin card 10 × 6in (25.5 × 15cm)
$\frac{1}{2}$yd (50cm) of $\frac{1}{2}$in (13mm) wide decorative
   braid
Lightweight wadding 12 × 7$\frac{1}{2}$in (30 × 19cm)
1$\frac{1}{4}$yd (1.1m) of $\frac{3}{8}$in (1cm) wide ribbon
Fabric adhesive
Matching sewing thread
Scissors and craft knife

To make étui

1 Cut out the card pieces as follows: From
thick card: four pieces **A** 4 × 3$\frac{1}{2}$in
(10 × 9cm); one piece **D** 3$\frac{1}{2}$in (9cm) square;
four pieces **E** 3 × 1$\frac{3}{4}$in (7.5 × 4.5cm); one
piece **H** 4 × 1in (10 × 2.5cm); two pieces **J**
7$\frac{3}{4}$ × 3$\frac{3}{4}$in (19.5 × 2cm) and one piece **K** 3$\frac{7}{8}$in
(9.8cm) square. From thin card: four pieces
B 3$\frac{3}{4}$ × 3$\frac{1}{4}$in (9.5 × 8cm); one piece **C** 3$\frac{1}{2}$in
(9cm) square; four pieces **F** 2$\frac{3}{4}$ × 1$\frac{1}{2}$in
(7 × 4cm); one piece **G** 1$\frac{3}{4}$in (4.5cm) square;
four pieces **I** $\frac{7}{8}$in (2cm) square; and one
piece **L** 3$\frac{3}{4}$in (9.5cm) square.

2 Using the card pieces as templates place
them on the fabric. Cut out each piece in
turn, adding $\frac{1}{2}$in (13mm) all round.

3 Using cards as templates, cut four pieces of
wadding the same size as card **B** and four
pieces the same size as card **F**.

4 Lay each piece of fabric **A** right side down
on a flat surface. Position card **A** to fabric.
Stick top and side edges to wrong side of
card. Stick base edges together to form flap.

5 Repeat, to cover pieces **B**, but stick a layer
of wadding to the card, before covering with
fabric. Stick all fabric edges to wrong side.

6 Cut the ribbon into 4in (10cm) lengths.
Stick $\frac{1}{2}$in (13mm) of ribbon centrally to the
back of each of the finished pieces **B**. Place
length of ribbon across the front and stick
remaining $\frac{1}{2}$in (13mm) in place at the back.
Pull the ribbon tight when glueing.

7 Cover the back of the finished piece **B**
with glue except for $\frac{1}{8}$in (3mm) round the
edge. Place this directly on top of the back
of finished piece **A**, leaving the base flap of
patterned fabric unstuck, flat on the table.
Cover with a heavy book and allow to dry.

8 Cover card **C** with fabric **C**, sticking all
four edges, turning neat corners. Leave to
dry.

9 Place **C** wrong side up on a flat surface.
Lay **AB** padded side down and stick the base
flap of patterned fabric to the wrong side of
C, keeping the two pieces close together.
AB should butt up against the square base
C. Repeat on the remaining three sides with
remaining pieces, leave to dry.

10 Cover card **D** with fabric **D** in the same
way as before, forming neat corners. Leave
to dry. Stick the whole of the wrong side of
D to within $\frac{1}{8}$in (3mm) of the edge and stick
pieces **C** and **D** with wrong sides together.
Cover with a heavy book and leave to dry.

11 Repeat, to make up pieces **E** in the same
way as for **A**. Repeat, to make up pieces **F** in
the same way as pieces **B**, adding 2$\frac{1}{4}$in
(5.5cm) lengths of ribbon. Stick **E** and **F**
together in the same way as **A** and **B**.

12 Cover card **G** with fabric **G**, sticking all
four sides. Stick four flaps of each piece **EF**
to wrong side of **G**. Leave to dry. Stick the
wrong side of **G** to within $\frac{1}{8}$in (3mm) of
edge and place on top of **C**.

13 Fold under each end of fabric **H**. Place
card side down on top of the fabric and stick
both long edges of fabric to the card to make
the thimble box, wrong side on inside.

14 Cover the four pieces of card **I** with fabric
pieces **I**, sticking all four sides. Slip these
four pieces into the inner faces of the box.
Apply the adhesive carefully to the base of
box and press firmly in place until dry.

15 Lay each card **J** onto the fabric. Tuck
both short ends of the fabric in to exactly
match the card edges, applying adhesive to
the long card edges and stick the fabric to
the card. Fold the length of card into a

square round card piece **K**, wrong side outwards. Sew two edges together with small hemming stitches.

16 Make the top piece using the card and fabric pieces **K**, sticking all four sides. Place the lid on top of the lid edge **J** and sew together with small hemming stitches. Make the lid

lining by covering card **L** with fabric **L**, stick all four sides. Apply adhesive to the underside of the lid **K** and push lining **L** into place.

17 Stick braid to the outer edge of the lid to cover remaining raw edges. Trim and seal braid so that the two raw edges butt together.

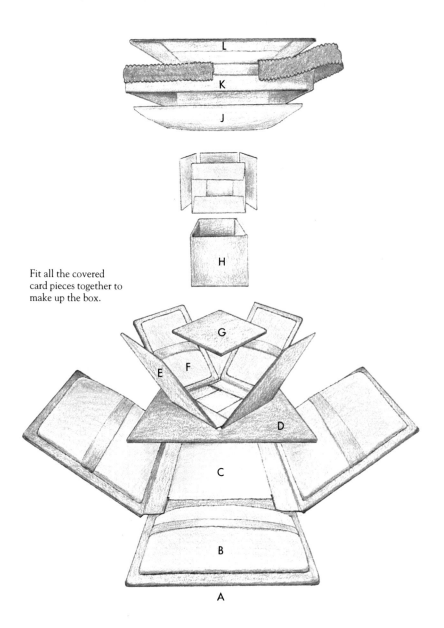

Fit all the covered card pieces together to make up the box.

Make-up bag

Keep your potions and lotions all zipped up in this little wash bag.
The outer fabric is a pretty printed cotton,
while inside there is a practical wipe-clean lining.
Make one to match your bedroom, bathroom or handbag,
or choose a nursery print to take care of baby's needs.

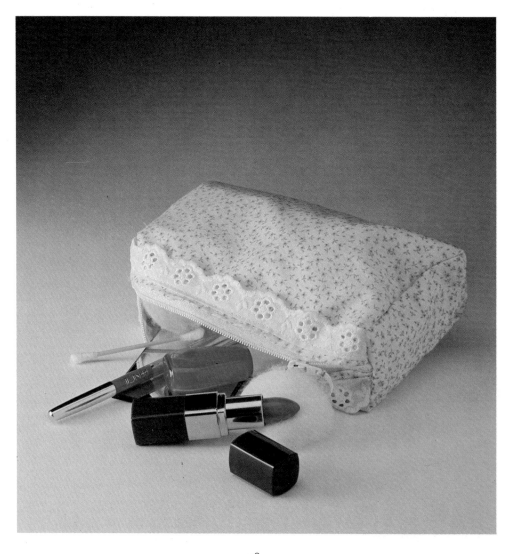

Materials
Printed cotton fabric 12in (30cm) square
Plastic lining the same size as fabric
8in (20cm) zip.
Small amount of $^1/_8$in (3mm) wide ribbon
$^1/_2$yd (50cm) of 1in (2.5cm) wide broderie
    anglaise trimming
Matching sewing thread

To make make-up bag
1 From printed fabric cut one piece 12×9in
(30×23cm). From plastic lining cut one
piece 11$^1/_2$×9in (29×23cm).

2 Lay the fabric piece right side down.
Position plastic lining centrally on top with
$^1/_4$in (6mm) protruding at either end. Stitch
all round close to outer edges.

3 Fold fabric over plastic lining at each side
and baste. Place these edges on either side of
zip. Pin, baste and stitch in place.

4 Place straight finished edge of broderie
anglaise along stitching lines on each side of
zip. Pin and topstitch in place. Open zip.

5 From fabric and plastic lining cut two side
pieces each 5$^1/_2$×3in (14×7.5cm). On one
short edge, turn under $^1/_4$in (6mm) then
place plastic lining to fabric with wrong sides
together. Stitch all round close to the outer
edge.

6 With right sides together, pin sides to
main bag, with neatened edges across zip
ends. Continue pinning down side edges,
snipping into corner diagonally to help turn
it neatly. Stitch all round, pivoting stitching
at base corners. Turn right side out.

7 Cut a 2in (5cm) length of ribbon. Thread
through the zip pull, knot and cut ends
diagonally.

You can make a 2in (5cm) tab of double
ribbon and insert it at the base of zip
between zip and side piece, to hold when
opening the zip.

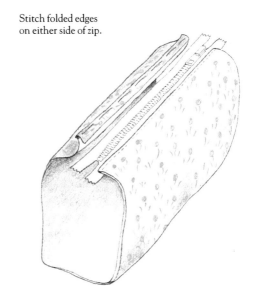

Stitch folded edges
on either side of zip.

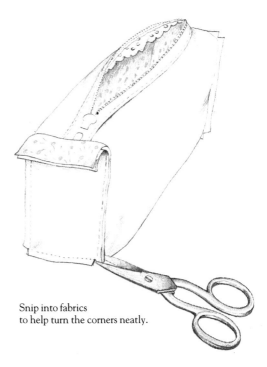

Snip into fabrics
to help turn the corners neatly.

Covered handsome hanger

*Take a simple wooden coat hanger and turn it into
a stunning gift for a favourite friend.
You can also add a matching pot pourri sachet to bring scent as well
as style to your wardrobe.*

Materials
Wooden coat hanger
Fabric 32×8in (81×20cm)
Wadding 18×4in (46×10cm)
Fabric adhesive
3½yd (3m) of ⅛in (3mm) wide satin ribbon
Small ribbon roses (optional)
Matching sewing thread

To make covered coat hanger
1 Place the hanger centrally on the wadding;
fold up wadding round the hanger, stretch it
slightly to mould into the hanger shape.
Trim to fit and stick to the hanger.

2 Fold the fabric evenly in half round the
hanger, with wrong side inside. Turn top
edges to the inside for ½in (13mm) and pin,
so there is about ¼in (6mm) free above pins.

3 To gather top edge of fabric, stitch along
¼in (6mm) from folded edge through both
thicknesses using a large machine stitch, and
working from the hook to both side edges.

4 Fasten off both ends of thread round hook.
Pull up from outer edges and gather up fabric
evenly along the hanger. Fasten off.

5 Fold ribbon in half and wrap centre point
round hook end. Add a spot of adhesive to
hold ribbon end. Wrap ribbon crisscross
over hook and along hanger working ends
back towards the hook. Tie ends in bow at
base of hook and secure with adhesive.

6 If desired, attach ribbon roses to the
ribbon intersections along top edge.

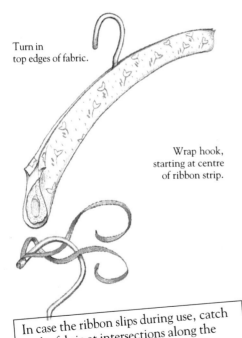

Turn in
top edges of fabric.

Wrap hook,
starting at centre
of ribbon strip.

In case the ribbon slips during use, catch
to the fabric at intersections along the
crossover effect.

Cotton wool holder

Make up a handy drawstring bag to keep cotton wool balls together.
The cords are long enough to tie into a loop to hang over
a bathroom hook or the back of a door.
A boon when travelling, you can make up larger bags
for shoes, hairdrier or tights and stockings.

Materials
Piece of printed fabric 17×6½in
    (43×16.5cm)
1⅜yd (1.3m) length of thin cord
Four toggles
Matching sewing thread

To make cotton wool holder
1 Fold fabric in half widthways with right
sides facing. Pin and stitch sides, taking ¼in
(6mm) seam allowance, to within 1in
(2.5cm) of top edge.

2 To form casing, turn down ½in (13mm) at
top edge and tuck under raw edge. Pin and

Work a bar tack by hand at top of
each side seam.

stitch along each casing. Tuck raw edges
inside casing at each end. Stitch a bar tack
at the top of side stitching.

3 Cut cord into two equal lengths. Thread
one piece of cord clockwise through casing,
thread on toggles and knot cord ends.

4 Thread second length of cord
anticlockwise through casing, thread on
toggles and knot cord ends, as before.

5 Pull up cords from each side to close bag.

61

Pot pourri sachet

Scent the whole room with sweet-smelling sachets.
Made in pretty print fabrics, these pot pourri sachets
can be hung in cupboards and slipped into linen drawers.

Materials
Printed cotton fabrics in a variety of colours
Pot pourri
Matching sewing thread
$^1/_8$ – $^1/_4$in (3–6mm) wide ribbon and $^1/_2$–$^3/_4$in
 (13–20mm) wide lace edging

To make pot pourri sachets
1 The larger sachets: cut out 9in (23cm)
diameter circles from fabric. The smaller
sachets: cut out 6$^1/_2$in (16.5cm) circles.

2 Measure the circumference of each circle
and cut a length of lace edging twice this
measurement. Gather up the straight lace
edge by hand.

3 Lay the fabric circle right side up, position
the lace with gathered edge overlapping the
outer edge of circle. Check that the gathers
are even, then pin and zigzag stitch the lace
in place, up to the join.

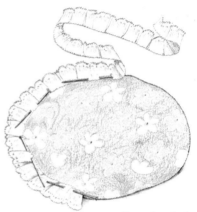

Pin gathered edging
all round fabric circle.

4 To join the lace edges, turn under raw
edges, so they just overlap. Trim off excess
lace, and continue stitching over the join.

5 Lay the fabric circle right side down; place
a small amount of pot pourri in the centre.
Gather up the fabric round the pot pourri
and hold in place by winding sewing thread
round the gathered-up fabric.

6 Loop ribbon round the sachet at thread
and tie in a bow. Cut ends diagonally.

7 Alternatively, use two lengths of different
coloured ribbon to tie up the sachet.

Use small plates or saucers as templates to
cut out the pot pourri sachets. Simply
place upside down on the wrong side of
the fabric and draw round.

Jewellery roll

This neat little roll-up will slip into a suitcase to provide
a storage place for your jewellery when travelling on holiday.
There's room for all your rings, brooches and necklaces.
Make one to match the make-up bag
for a co-ordinated travel kit.

Materials
Printed fabric 36 × 17in (91 × 43cm)
Mediumweight iron-on interfacing
    19¹/₂ × 6¹/₂in (49.5 × 16.5cm)
Three white press studs
Six small press fasteners
Small amount of cotton wool
Scrap of lightweight wadding
Matching sewing thread

To make jewellery roll
1 For the main piece cut two pieces of fabric
19¹/₂ × 6¹/₂in (49.5 × 16.5cm). Fuse
interfacing to wrong side of one fabric piece.

2 For the flap pocket cut a piece of fabric
7¹/₂ × 5in (19 × 12.5cm). Fold in half
widthways; tuck under ¹/₂in (13mm) along
raw edges. Cut a piece of wadding to the size
of folded fabric and place inside folded
fabric; baste together all round. Topstitch
across top edge.

3 Position pocket centrally 2in (5cm) up
from one short edge on interfaced fabric; pin
and topstitch in place close to outer edge on
three sides.

4 Make a pocket flap, cut two pieces of
fabric each 5¹/₂ × 4in (14 × 10cm). Place with
wrong sides together. Stitch sides for 1in
(2.5cm) then down to centre in a V shape.
Trim and turn right side out; press.
Topstitch pointed edges. Turn in remaining
straight edge for ¹/₂in (13mm); pin and baste.
Position above pocket; topstitch in place
across top straight edge.

5 Form pad by positioning a piece of
wadding 4¹/₂ × 3in (11 × 7.5cm) behind
interfaced fabric 1¹/₂ (4cm) up from pocket.
Pin and zigzag stitch in place.

6 Make a square flap over pad, by cutting
two pieces of fabric each 5³/₄ × 4¹/₂in
(14.5 × 11.5cm). Turn in ¹/₂in (13mm)
round all edges. Place with wrong sides
together, matching folded edges. Pin and
topstitch one long and both short sides.
Position over padded section and topstitch
across remaining long edge to stitch it to
background.

7 Make a ring holder by cutting a piece of
fabric 6 × 1¹/₂in (15 × 4cm). Fold in half
lengthways; pin and stitch edges taking ¹/₄in
(6mm) seam allowance. Turn right side out.
Fill with cotton wool, tuck under raw edges
at each end and stitch to close. Position ¹/₂in
(13mm) above padded section; stitch down
one end. Fasten opposite end in place with
press stud.

8 Cut two pieces of fabric 12¹/₂ × 1³/₄in
(31.5 × 4.5cm) for straps. Fold each strap in
half lengthways. Pin and stitch long edges,
taking ¹/₄in (6mm) seam allowance. Turn
right side out. Turn in short edges, pin and
topstitch all round strap.

9 Fold each strap in half and fix a press stud
to fasten ends. Sew three press fasteners
along each strap, spaced ¹/₂in (13mm) apart,
in from stud.

10 Position the base half of each strap 1¹/₄in
(3cm) in from opposite side edge of
background fabric, and 2in (5cm) apart. Pin
and topstitch in place, leaving second half
free, to fold over and fasten in place. Fix
opposite halves of all fasteners to
background.

11 Cut a piece of fabric 32 × 2¹/₄in
(81 × 5.5cm) for fastening strap. Fold in half
with right sides together. Pin and stitch raw
edges together, taking ¹/₄in (6mm) seam
allowance and leaving a gap in the centre for
turning. Trim across corners and turn right
side out. Turn in opening edges in line with
remainder of the seam and slipstitch
together to close. Topstitch round strap.
Fold strap in half and position fold centrally
at end of interfaced backing, fastening
inwards.

12 Place interfaced backing with right side
to plain backing. Pin, tack and stitch
together all round, taking ¹/₂in (13mm) seam
allowance and leaving a gap in the centre in
one side for turning. Trim across corners and
turn right side out. Turn in open edges in
line with remainder of the seam and
slipstitch together to close. Topstitch all
round roll.

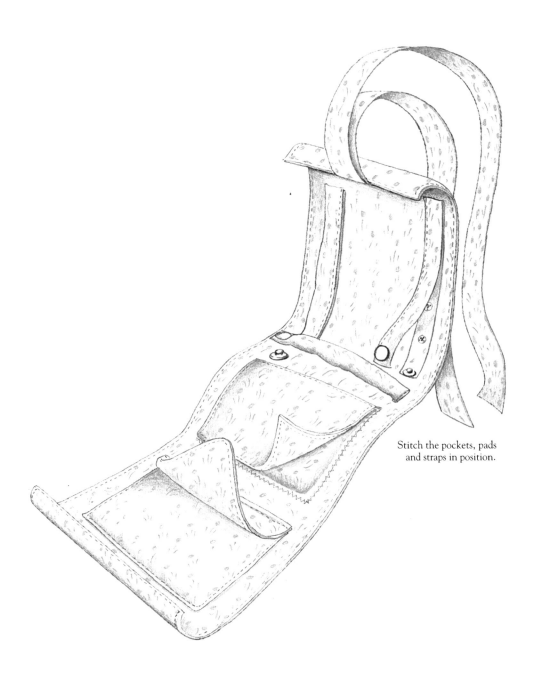

Stitch the pockets, pads
and straps in position.

Place mats

Lay a stylish table with bright gingham table mats.
They'll protect your table as well as give it a cheery look.
There is a serving mat as well, for hot vegetable dishes.
Make both sides of the mat in the same fabric
or choose contrasting fabrics to double their use.

Materials

For two two place mats and one serving mat:
$^3/_4$yd (70cm) of 36in (90cm) wide gingham
Mediumweight wadding 32 × 22in
(81 × 56cm)
$4^1/_4$yd (4m) of 1in (2.5cm) wide bias binding
Matching sewing threads

You can make up your binding from another fabric by simply cutting out bias strips and pressing them through a tape and binder maker.

To make place mats

1 For one place mat, cut two pieces of fabric each 12$^1/_2$ × 9in (31.5 × 23cm) and one piece of wadding the same size.

2 Place two fabric pieces with wrong sides together, sandwiching a piece of wadding in between. Pin and baste together round the outer edges and at regular intervals across the fabric, to hold the three pieces firmly together.

3 Using a long stitch on the sewing machine, diagonally quilt across the fabric. Begin by working one row across the centre from corner to corner, then work a line centrally across the mat in the opposite direction. Continue working quilting lines, on each side of first lines, 1$^1/_2$in (4cm) apart.

4 To round off the corners, place a small plate to one corner so sides of plate match fabric edges and mark round. Trim off corner. Use this corner as a template for trimming the remaining corners to match.

5 Press bias binding evenly in half. Place edge of mat inside folded bias binding. Begin centrally in one long side; pin, baste and topstitch binding in place. At end, tuck under raw edge of binding and overlap raw edge for $^1/_2$in (13mm).

6 Make up second mat in the same way.

7 For serving mat, cut two pieces of fabric and two pieces of wadding to 15$^1/_2$ × 12$^1/_2$in (39 × 31.5cm).

8 Make up serving mat in the same way, inserting two layers of wadding in between the fabric pieces, and quilt across the mat in 3in (7.5cm) squares.

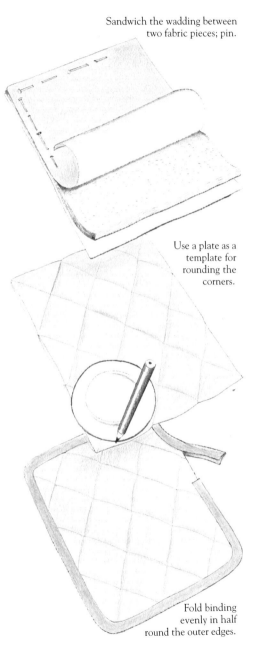

Sandwich the wadding between two fabric pieces; pin.

Use a plate as a template for rounding the corners.

Fold binding evenly in half round the outer edges.

Napkin rings

Avoid confusion at family meal times by making everyone a personalized napkin ring. We chose to make ours to match the gingham place mats, but you could make up a set of rings in different colours, so that everyone will be able to recognize their own napkin. Add ribbon roses or ready-made embroidered initials to trim.

Materials for two rings:
Cylinder of card from aluminium foil roll
Off-cuts of gingham fabric from place mats
Spray adhesive
⁷/₈yd (90cm) of ³/₈in (1cm) wide ribbon
Four small ribbon roses

To make napkin rings
1 Cut cylinder into two 1¹/₄in (3cm) lengths.

2 Measure round cylinder and cut a piece of fabric to this measurement plus 1in (2.5cm) for overlap, by the length of the cylinder plus 1¹/₂in (4cm).

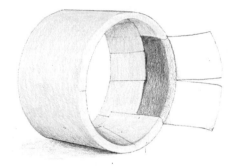

Stick the overlaps to the inside on both edges.

3 Place fabric right side down, spray with adhesive and place cylinder in the centre. Smooth fabric round cylinder, overlapping edges. Trim overlap on one end to ¹/₂in (13mm). Snip overlap at sides at ¹/₂in (13mm) intervals; stick to inside of ring. Repeat, with other side.

4 Make up second ring in the same way.

5 Cut ribbon in half. Tie each half into a bow. Stick bow and two ribbon roses over seam on each napkin ring. Cut ends of ribbon diagonally.

Check the size and thickness of the card cylinders before you cut out your rings, as they do vary in size.

Curtain call

*Tie-backs add the finishing touch to curtains
and can be decorated with ruffles and trimmings to match the room:
plain, crisp-edged tie-backs with modern looks,
while ruffled tie-backs look best in chintzy rooms.*

Materials

Furnishing cotton and heavyweight iron-on
    interfacing, see below for amounts
Four ³/₄in (2cm) diameter curtain rings for
    each pair of tie-backs
Paper for pattern
Lace edging (see below for amount)
Matching sewing thread

To make tie-backs

1 Hold a tape measure round the pulled back
curtain to gauge the length of the tie back.
On a doubled sheet of paper draw a rectangle
to half this length by the chosen width,
matching one short edge to fold of paper.
Draw the shaped lines of the tie-back
freehand. Keeping the paper folded, cut out
the pattern. Check the size and shape by
pinning round the curtain.

2 Using pattern, cut out four tie-back shapes
from fabric, adding ⁵/₈in (1.5cm) seam
allowance all round. Cut two pieces of
interfacing the same size as the pattern.

3 Fuse one piece of interfacing centrally to
wrong side of one fabric tie-back. Repeat for
second tie-back.

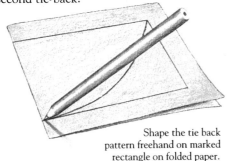

Shape the tie back
pattern freehand on marked
rectangle on folded paper.

4 Measure curved edge of tie-back and cut
lace edging for each tie-back to twice this
length. Turn under a narrow double hem at
each end of edging; pin and stitch. Gather
up top edge of edging to fit base edge of tie-
back. Position edging to right side of
interfaced tie-back, with gathering to
seamline and with lace facing inwards. Pin
and baste in place.

5 Match together interfaced tie-backs to
plain tie-backs with right sides together.
Pin, tack and stitch together all round,
leaving an opening in one side. Trim and
turn to right side. Turn in open edges in line
with remainder of seam, slipstitch together.

6 Handsew a curtain ring to the top point of
each tie-back.

Oven mitt

Bring food from the oven to table in safety with a practical oven mitt.
Made from stout cotton with layers of wadding for insulation,
the mitt is good to look at too.
We added a tape loop so you can hang your mitt near the oven.
Why not make two mitts so you'll be well covered in a hot situation?

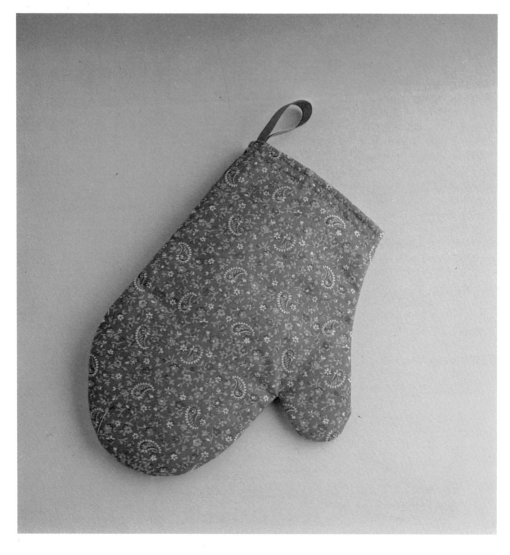

Materials

Paper for pattern
Printed fabric 24 × 10in (61 × 25.5cm)
Plain cotton fabric the same size for lining
Mediumweight wadding 24 × 20in
 (61 × 51cm)
7in (18cm) of ¹/₂in (13mm) wide tape
Matching sewing thread

To make the oven mitt

1 Lay your hand on a sheet of paper with the fingers spread apart. Draw freehand round the hand in a rounded mitt shape. Remove hand and cut out the pattern. Check the size – the finished mitt should be about 11in (28cm) long and about 8¹/₂in (21.5cm) at the widest part.

2 Using pattern, cut two pieces from printed fabric, two from plain fabric and four pieces of wadding, adding ¹/₂in (13mm) all round.

3 Pin and baste a piece of wadding to wrong side of each printed fabric mitt.

4 Place wadded mitt pieces with right sides together; pin, baste and stitch together all round curved edge, leaving wrist edges open. Turn under wrist edges and baste. Turn right side out.

5 Pin and baste wadding to plain mitt shapes and seam together in the same way. Turn under wrist edges and baste.

6 Slip plain fabric mitt inside printed fabric mitt with wadded sides together, matching wrist edges together.

7 Fold tape into a 3in (7.5cm) loop. Fit between the two layers at back of mitt. Pin, tack and topstitch round wrist edges, with two rows of stitching.

8 Make a couple of handstitches through top of mitt to hold the print and plain lining layers together.

You could cut the lining sections from reflective curtain lining to help deflect the heat.

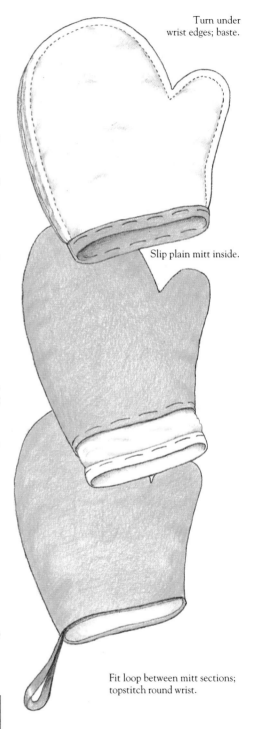

Turn under wrist edges; baste.

Slip plain mitt inside.

Fit loop between mitt sections; topstitch round wrist.

Star bright

*Make a Victorian-style patchwork star in three different fabrics
to hang up as an ornament.
Change the fabrics to baby prints to make an alternative to a mobile,
or small Christmas fabrics for a festive decoration.
The points are finished with crystals and pearls.*

Materials
30 × 5in (76 × 12.5cm) each of three print
    fabrics
Card 15 × 8in (38 × 20cm)
1¼in (3cm) lozenge diamond patchwork
    template
Matching sewing thread
Fabric adhesive
1¼yd (1.2m) of ⅜in (1cm) wide ribbon
20 pins
Ten matching pearl beads
20 pearl beads
20 crystal beads

To make the star
1 Using the template, cut out sixty
diamonds from card.

2 Place fabric pieces wrong side up. Mark
round diamond template 20 times on each
fabric, allowing a ½in (13mm) margin all
round each one. Cut out the diamonds.

3 Place each fabric diamond right side down
and stick card diamond centrally to each
piece. Carefully pull raw edges over card
edge and stick to wrong side.

4 Mixing the fabrics, stitch five diamonds
together to form a rosette. To sew the
diamonds together, place with right sides
together and work along one side with
hemming stitch. Open out. Hem third
diamond to second diamond and repeat,
until five diamonds are joined together.

5 Following the instructions in step 4 above, make another eleven rosettes of five diamonds. (You will now have twelve.)

6 Stitch a single pearl bead into centre of ten rosettes.

7 Cut two 12in (30cm) lengths of ribbon. Match together. Fold in half to form loops, push ends through centre of one plain rosette and fasten on the wrong side. This will be the base rosette.

8 Form a loop with the remaining ribbon, push through centre of last plain rosette and fasten on wrong side. This will be the top rosette.

9 Take the base rosette and sew a rosette to each pair of sides. Then sew the rosettes together round the side edges. Repeat, to make up the top rosette in the same way. Note: you will now have to sew from the outside.

11 Sew the top and base halves together, along the remaining free edges, again using small hemming stitches.

12 Thread a pearl bead and then crystal bead onto each pin and pin into each of the twenty points in turn on the star.

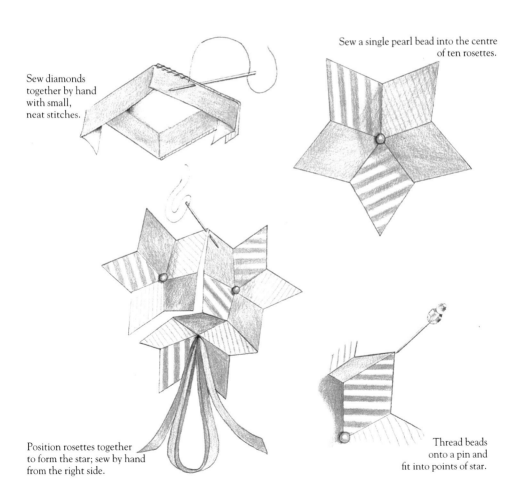

Sew diamonds together by hand with small, neat stitches.

Sew a single pearl bead into the centre of ten rosettes.

Position rosettes together to form the star; sew by hand from the right side.

Thread beads onto a pin and fit into points of star.

Baby quilt

The perfect gift for the mother-to-be or for a newborn baby.
The patchwork design is called Baby Blocks,
made up of three diamonds arranged to look like a child's building block.
The completed patchwork is hand quilted to give
a raised relief effect to the whole design.

Materials
40 × 10in (102 × 25cm) piece of cotton fabric
 in each of three different designs, plus
 extra for border strips
2¹/₂in (6cm) lozenge diamond template
Paper for backing patchwork shapes
Mediumweight wadding and piece of plain
 cotton for backing each 30 × 37in
 (76 × 94cm)
Buttonhole thread, for quilting
Matching sewing thread

To make the patchwork quilt
1 Using the patchwork template cut out a
paper shape for each of the 93 diamonds.

2 Using template mark out diamonds on the
wrong side of each fabric, allowing an extra
¹/₄in (6mm) all round each piece. Cut out
each shape.

3 Position a paper shape centrally to wrong
side of fabric shape, pin in position.

4 Turn the seam allowance over the paper
backing on each side of the diamond in turn;
baste in place through paper shape.

5 To form each block, position a set of three
diamonds as shown, with one diamond
turned sideways over two more diamonds.
Make up as many blocks as you need for the
quilt – this quilt has seven rows of 4¹/₂
blocks.

6 To sew the blocks together, place two diamonds with right sides together and oversew the matched edges together exactly.

7 Once you have made up your blocks, stitch them together into the size of the quilt centre. As the patchwork centre has straight edges it will be necessary to have half blocks, in alternate rows.

8 Once the patchwork is finished, measure the length and cut two pieces each 3³/₄in (9.5cm) wide for border strips. Pin, baste and stitch strips first to side edges, taking ¹/₄in (6mm) seam allowance on patchwork and ¹/₂in (13mm) seam on border strip. Trim and press flat. Then pin and stitch border strips to top and lower edges in the same way. Trim and press flat.

9 Add a second border in the same way.

10 Cut a piece of wadding to size of quilt and pin and baste to wrong side, round outer edges and across quilt at regular intervals.

11 Using buttonhole thread, quilt by hand, taking small running stitches round the patchwork shapes and to form a diagonal design along the border sections.

12 After quilting, place the patchwork with right side to backing fabric; pin and stitch together all round, leaving an opening in lower edge, for turning. Trim and turn quilt to the right side. Turn in opening edges in line with the remainder of the seam and slipstitch together to close.

13 Anchor backing to quilted front by quilting round the quilt in between patchwork and the first and second border strips.

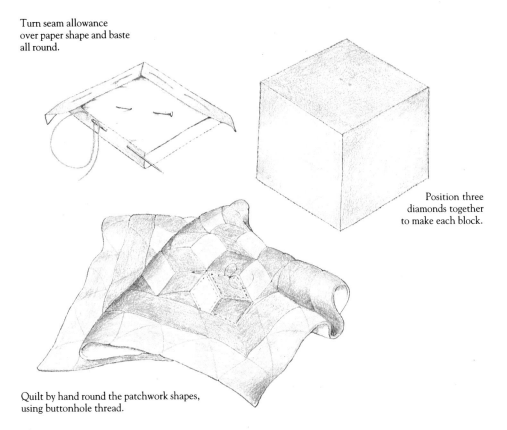

Turn seam allowance over paper shape and baste all round.

Position three diamonds together to make each block.

Quilt by hand round the patchwork shapes, using buttonhole thread.